For **Eigil**, **Erik** and **Nanna**
I hope you'll get to explore
Scotland for yourselves one day.
—A.F.

THIS BOOK BELONGS TO

MADE IN SCOTLAND

This book was handcrafted in Scotland. It was created by Edinburgh-based
illustrator Anders Frang and the team at Floris Books, an independent
Edinburgh publisher, and printed in Glasgow.

Kelpies is an imprint of Floris Books. First published in 2020 by Floris Books
Second printing 2022. Text © 2020 Floris Books. Illustrations © 2020 Anders Frang
Anders Frang has asserted his right under the Copyright, Designs and Patent Act 1988
to be identified as the Illustrator of this Work. All rights reserved No part of this
book may be reproduced without the prior permission of Floris Books, Edinburgh
www.florisbooks.co.uk British Library CIP data available
ISBN 978-178250-659-1 Printed in Great Britain by Bell & Bain Ltd

Printed on sustainably
sourced FSC® certified
paper. Uses plant-based
inks which reduces
chemical emissions.

FSC
www.fsc.org
MIX
From responsible
sources
FSC® C007785

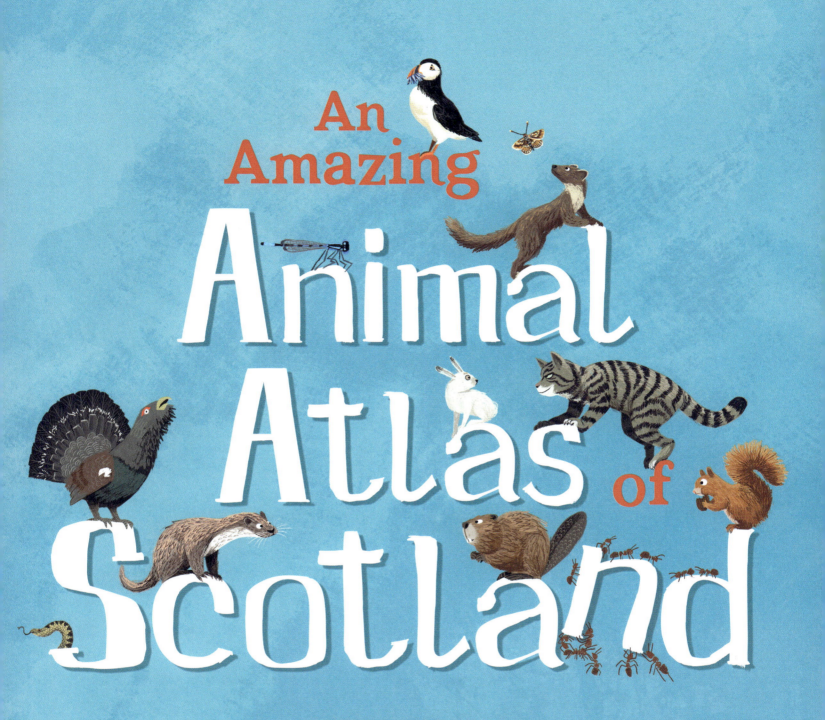

An Amazing Animal Atlas of Scotland

Illustrated by
Anders Frang

Kelpies
World

Welcome to Scotland

MOUNTAINS and FORESTS

Britain's highest mountains and biggest forests are in Scotland. These remote places are a great home for the country's most endangered species.

page 18

SEA and COAST

Three quarters of Britain's seabirds nest on Scottish shores.

page 8

Shetland Islands

Orkney Islands

Aberdeen

Inverness

Loch Ness

Lewis and Harris

Skye

Uist

St Kilda

Atlantic Ocean

GRASSLANDS

page 36

Scotland's hillsides and meadows are home to animals like Highland cows and Shetland ponies, which are happy in cold, wet weather.

RIVERS AND LOCHS

page 28

Loch is the Scottish word for lake. Scotland's lochs and rivers are home to otters, beavers and salmon.

SUPPORT SCOTTISH ANIMALS

page 42

Explore the coast and countryside, learn more about endangered species, and find easy ways to support wildlife with our top tips.

North Sea

England

Dundee

Edinburgh (Scotland's capital city)

Loch Lomond

Glasgow (Scotland's biggest city)

Mull

Jura

Islay

Arran

Irish Sea

Wales

Northern Ireland

Republic of Ireland

Sea and Coast

Scotland has over 800 islands, but people only live on 118 of them.

Scotland's beaches and sand dunes make up three quarters of the sand in Britain!

MORAY FIRTH

Bottlenose dolphins swim so close to the shore in the Moray Firth, you can see them from land.

ORKNEY ISLANDS

25,000 grey seals and 7,000 common seals live on the Orkney Islands. It's easiest to spot them on beaches in October when grey seals have their pups.

ST KILDA

The tiny islands of St Kilda are the most remote in Britain. People lived here until 1930 and used to climb the high cliffs to catch seabirds for food. Now St Kilda is home to 1 million seabirds!

North Sea

Atlantic Ocean

Irish Sea

BASS ROCK

150,000 gannets nest on Bass Rock, making it the biggest single colony in the world. It looks white because of all their poo!

Two thirds of Britain's fish and seafood is caught in the seas around Scotland.

The wiggly Scottish coastline is 18,000 kilometres long – that's the distance from Scotland to Australia!

Many of Scotland's lochs are fresh water, but sea lochs are salt water with tides.

WHERE TO SPOT

Seal

Orca

Sea eagle

Puffin

Gannet

Dolphin

Basking shark

Minke whale

Deep Sea Swimmers

SUPERHERO SWIMMERS

Bottlenose dolphins are among the cleverest animals in the world. They sometimes rescue people from drowning.

BUSY BRAINS

Dolphins always have to swim to the surface to breathe, which means they never fully sleep!

TEETH-TASTIC

Common dolphins have 80–100 sharp pointed teeth on each jaw, which they use to grip fish before swallowing them whole.

STAR SPOT

MASSIVE MINKE

A fully grown minke whale can be 10 metres long – that's as wide as a cinema screen.

SONIC SATNAV

Dolphins and whales make high-pitched clicking sounds to find their way around. When the soundwaves hit an object, they bounce back as echoes, which tell whales and dolphins the object's size, shape and location. This clever process is called 'echolocation'.

SHARING SNACKS

If you see seabirds feasting, a whale might be close by, driving fish towards the surface.

SUPER SCOOPER

Minke whales chase shoals of fish with their huge mouths open wide.

PIG-POISE

The harbour porpoise is a smaller, more shy member of the dolphin family. It makes a puffing sound when it breathes and is known as a 'puffing pig'.

Seabird Cities

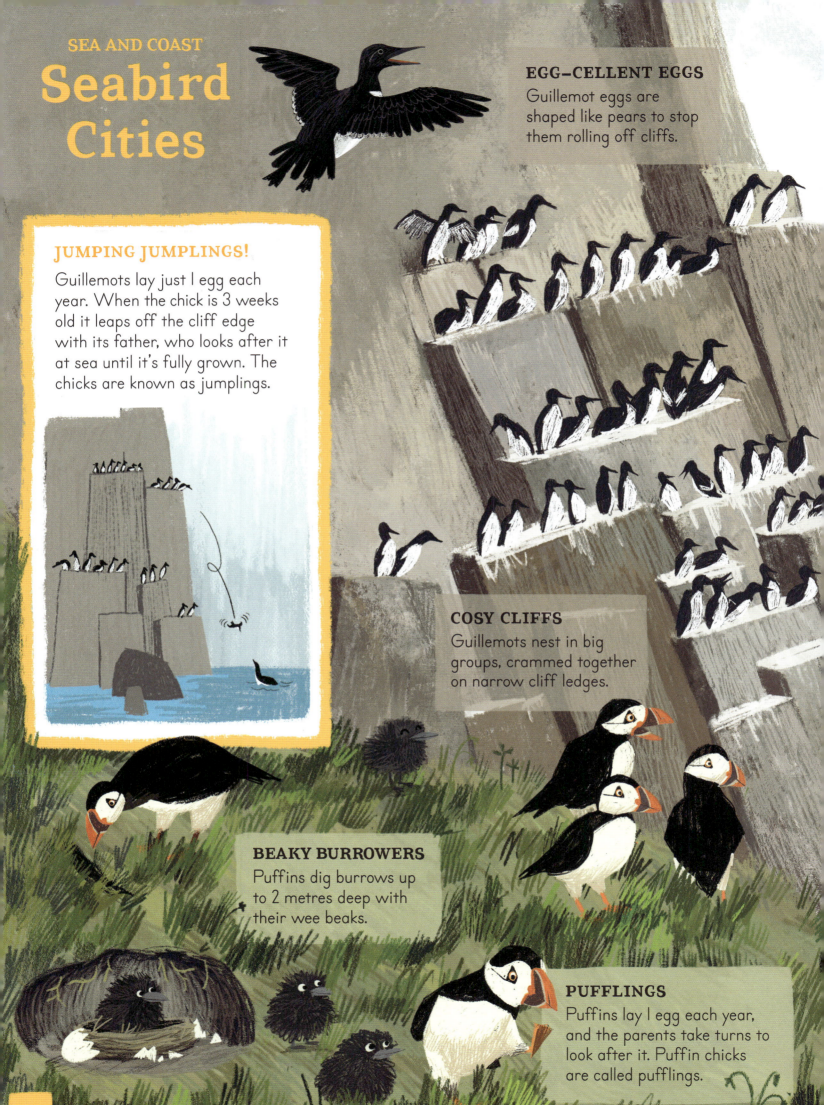

EGG–CELLENT EGGS
Guillemot eggs are shaped like pears to stop them rolling off cliffs.

JUMPING JUMPLINGS!
Guillemots lay just 1 egg each year. When the chick is 3 weeks old it leaps off the cliff edge with its father, who looks after it at sea until it's fully grown. The chicks are known as jumplings.

COSY CLIFFS
Guillemots nest in big groups, crammed together on narrow cliff ledges.

BEAKY BURROWERS
Puffins dig burrows up to 2 metres deep with their wee beaks.

PUFFLINGS
Puffins lay 1 egg each year, and the parents take turns to look after it. Puffin chicks are called pufflings.

12

SKY HIGH HUNTERS

Sea eagles mostly eat fish, as well as other birds, rabbits, hares and even lambs!

STAR SPOT

SUPREME SEA EAGLE

The sea (or white-tailed) eagle is the biggest bird of prey in Britain. It has a wingspan of 2 ½ metres and is known as the 'flying barn door'. Sea eagles were once hunted to extinction in Britain, but they were reintroduced and now around 250 nest in Scotland.

SPECTACULAR SWOOPERS

Gannets dive head first into the sea from 30 metres — as high as the Kelpies sculptures near Falkirk! They hit the water at speeds of 60 miles per hour — as fast as a car on the motorway.

LIGHT-WEIGHT

A puffin weighs the same as a can of fizzy drink!

GANNET LAND

Nearly half a million gannets nest in Scotland — that's most of the world's gannets and the same as the number of people who live in Edinburgh.

Coastal Creatures

MOO-VELLOUS SEALS
Male seals are called bulls. Female seals are called cows.

AWESOME ORCA
The orca (or killer whale) is actually the biggest member of the dolphin family. It can grow up to 8 metres – the length of a double-decker bus! Only a few live in the seas around Scotland, but others come to visit.

STAR SPOT

SEAL STALKER
Orcas live in groups called pods and hunt together. They eat fish, porpoises and seals, but no animals eat them.

FLUFFY PUPS
When they are born, grey seal pups weigh the same as a human toddler. They stay on land until they have shed all their white fluff and weigh the same as a 12-year-old child!

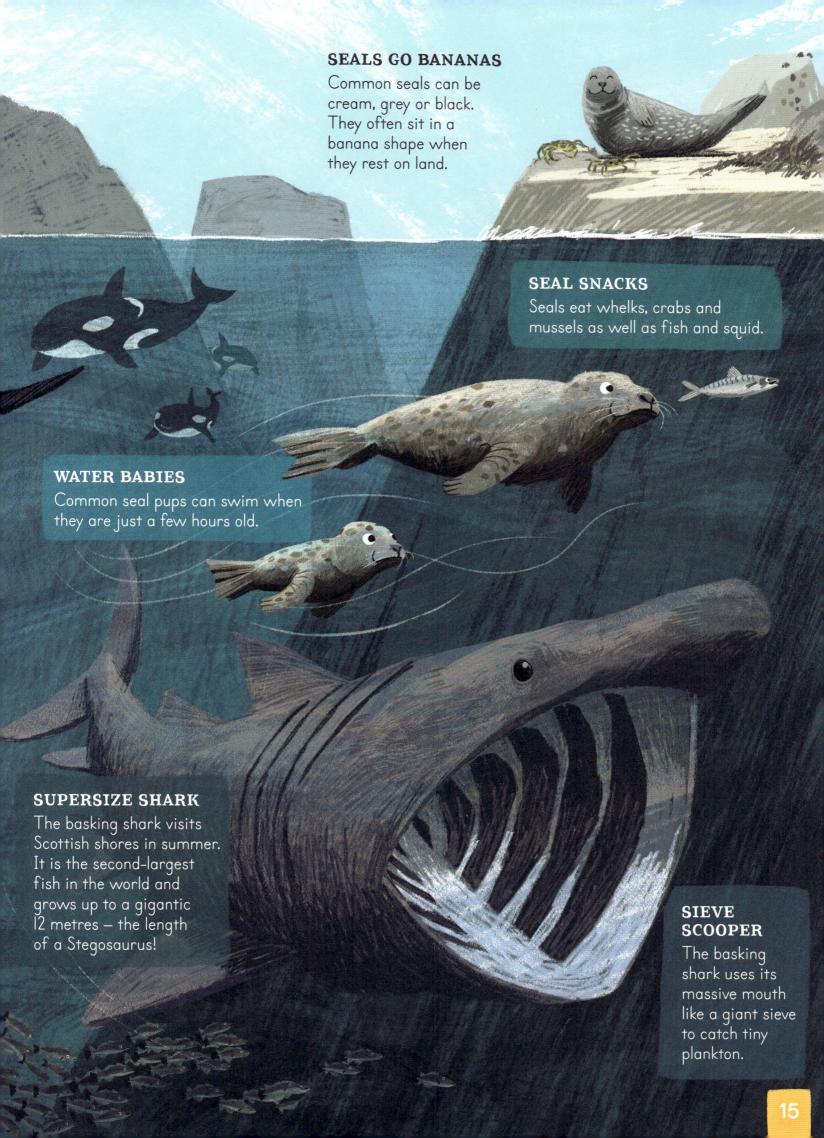

SEALS GO BANANAS
Common seals can be cream, grey or black. They often sit in a banana shape when they rest on land.

SEAL SNACKS
Seals eat whelks, crabs and mussels as well as fish and squid.

WATER BABIES
Common seal pups can swim when they are just a few hours old.

SUPERSIZE SHARK
The basking shark visits Scottish shores in summer. It is the second-largest fish in the world and grows up to a gigantic 12 metres – the length of a Stegosaurus!

SIEVE SCOOPER
The basking shark uses its massive mouth like a giant sieve to catch tiny plankton.

Rockpool Raiders

CHATTY CRABS

Shore crabs communicate with each other by drumming or waving their pincers.

WHAT'S THAT BLOB?

Above water, beadlet anemones pull in their tentacles and look like blobs of jelly.

FABULOUS FILTERS

Blue mussels open up underwater to feed on plankton, which they sieve out of the water. They get through 100 pints a day. That's one child's school milk for a year!

TRAPPING TENTACLES

Underwater, beadlet anemones use their stinging tentacles to catch passing shrimps, crabs or small fish.

STAR URCHIN?

Starfish are not actually fish. They are a type of sea urchin. If they lose an arm, they can grow it back!

STAR SPOT

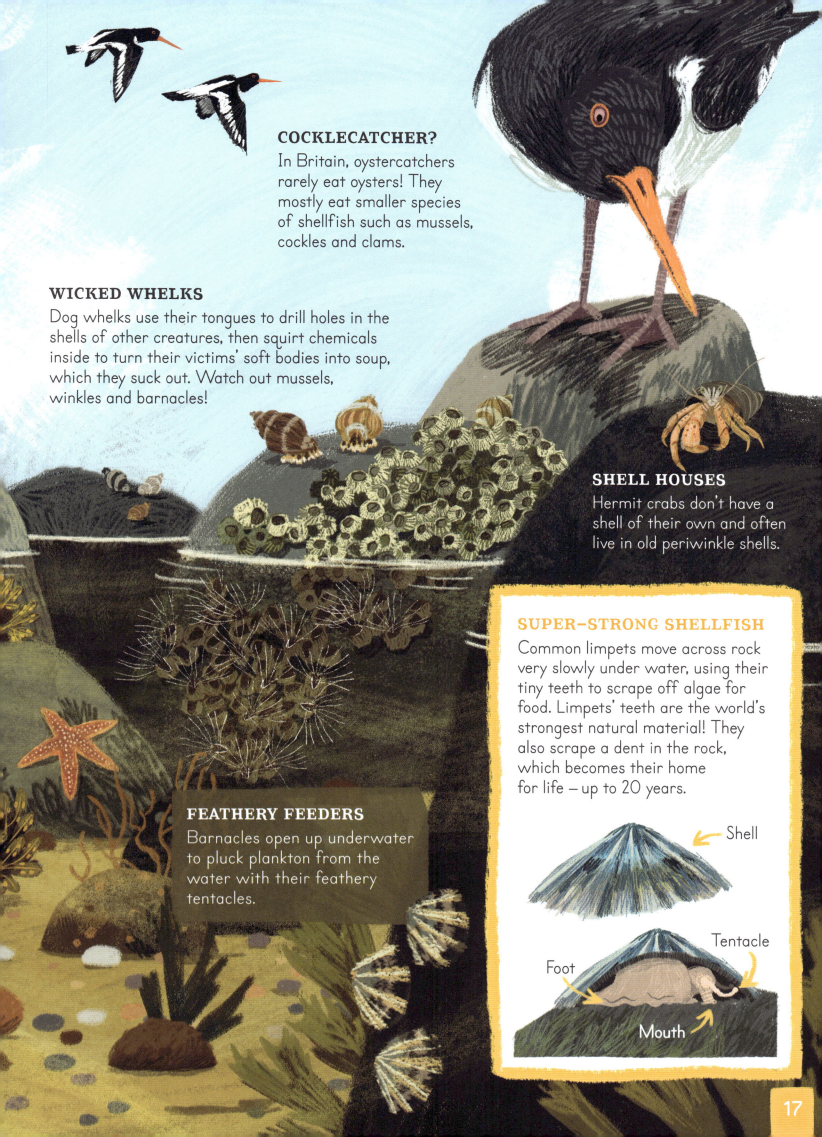

COCKLECATCHER?

In Britain, oystercatchers rarely eat oysters! They mostly eat smaller species of shellfish such as mussels, cockles and clams.

WICKED WHELKS

Dog whelks use their tongues to drill holes in the shells of other creatures, then squirt chemicals inside to turn their victims' soft bodies into soup, which they suck out. Watch out mussels, winkles and barnacles!

SHELL HOUSES

Hermit crabs don't have a shell of their own and often live in old periwinkle shells.

SUPER-STRONG SHELLFISH

Common limpets move across rock very slowly under water, using their tiny teeth to scrape off algae for food. Limpets' teeth are the world's strongest natural material! They also scrape a dent in the rock, which becomes their home for life – up to 20 years.

Shell

Tentacle

Foot

Mouth

FEATHERY FEEDERS

Barnacles open up underwater to pluck plankton from the water with their feathery tentacles.

Mountains and Forests

The trees and plants in Scottish forests absorb lots of carbon dioxide, helping to reduce pollution and climate change.

The summit of Britain's highest mountain, Ben Nevis, is 1,345 metres (4,411 feet) above sea level – that's nearly a mile high.

CAIRNGORMS NATIONAL PARK

A quarter of Britain's endangered animals live in the remote mountains and forests of the Cairngorms National Park. Some of them don't live in any other part of the world.

NORTHWEST HIGHLANDS

CALEDONIAN FOREST

After the Ice Age, nearly 10,000 years ago, a huge forest of pine trees covered Scotland. Now only patches of this ancient forest remain in parts of the Highlands. The soil, plants and animals found there are different from anywhere else in the world.

There are 282 mountains over 3,000 feet (914.4 metres) high in Scotland. They are called Munros, after the man who first measured and counted them all.

The highest 75 mountains in Britain are in Scotland.

GALLOWAY FOREST

This huge forest is a massive 300 square miles – that's 3 times the size of Edinburgh. Visit the forest to see red deer roaring, red squirrels leaping and red kites soaring through the sky.

Three quarters of the forest and woodland in Britain is in Scotland.

Ben Nevis

HIGHLANDS

WHERE TO SPOT

Golden eagle

Red kite

Wildcat

Mountain hare

Red deer

Capercaillie

Pine marten

Red squirrel

ISLE OF MULL

This hilly island is the best place in Britain to see both golden eagles and sea eagles. Bird watchers call it Eagle Island.

Sky Hunters

STAR SPOT

GLORIOUS GOLDEN EAGLE

The golden eagle is the second-largest bird of prey in Britain, with a wingspan of over 2 metres — that's the size of a sofa! It is extinct everywhere in Britain except for the Highlands of Scotland.

PLUNGING PREDATOR

The golden eagle soars high in the sky, then dives as fast as 150 miles per hour — that's even faster than a train. It hunts rabbits, mountain hares, grouse, foxes and young deer, but nothing eats it.

PIGEON PUNCHING

The peregrine falcon hunts smaller birds like wood pigeons by punching them with its talons as it dives.

SWOOPING SCAVENGERS

Red kites often line their nests with sheep's wool, paper, plastic and cloth — even old socks!

RED KITES RETURN

Red kites nearly became extinct in Britain because of their eggs being stolen and illegal poisoning. They were reintroduced 30 years ago and now 1,600 breeding pairs live in Britain.

FAST FALCON

The peregrine falcon is the speediest bird in the world. It dives as fast as 200 miles per hour – that's the top speed of a Ferrari.

BIRD BUILDERS

Golden eagles build giant nests called 'eyries' on rocky outcrops or in trees, which are used for many years by lots of eagle families.

CAT CALL

The buzzard is the most common bird of prey in Britain. Its call sounds like a cat's miaow.

Majestic Mountains

SPOTTY SIBLINGS

Roe deer live all over Scotland, even on the outskirts of cities. Females usually have twin fawns once a year, but sometimes they have triplets.

STRUT YOUR STUFF

Male black grouse fluff up their tail feathers, dance around and sing to attract females.

SNOW SHOES

The mountain hare's broad paws act like skis to stop it sinking into the snow.

STAR SPOT

HOPPING MOUNTAIN HARE

Scotland's native hare now only lives in the high mountains, after brown hares and rabbits took over its habitat. Its numbers are also shrinking because of hunting.

CLEVER CAMOUFLAGE

In summer, both the mountain hare and the ptarmigan change colour from white to grey-brown to match the moorland landscape around them.

AMAZING ANTLERS
Red deer stags have huge antlers that drop off in spring and grow back in summer. Their antlers get bigger every year and can weigh 15 kilograms, the same as a 2-year-old child.

STAG SKIRMISH
Red deer stags fight to win herds of females. They clash their huge antlers and roar.

SNOW CHICKENS
In Britain the ptarmigan (pronounced tar-mi-gun) only lives in the Scottish Highlands because it prefers cold, icy, mountain landscapes. In the USA, ptarmigans are called snow chickens!

Fascinating Forests

MYSTERIOUS MARTEN

Pine martens are very shy and usually come out at night, which makes them difficult to spot.

SUPER SCOTTISH SPECIES

You can't see a Scottish crossbill anywhere else in the world! Its special beak is perfect for picking seeds out of pine, spruce and larch cones.

ASTOUNDING ANTS

Scottish wood ants only live in the Highlands. Their colonies are mostly underground and a single colony may contain over 100,000 ants.

ANT ACID!

Soldier ants squirt formic acid at attackers. It smells like salt and vinegar crisps!

24

RARE RED SQUIRREL

Red squirrels are native to Britain. When bigger grey squirrels were introduced from America 150 years ago, they took over the food supply and woodlands, and brought a deadly virus called squirrelpox. There's only 1 red squirrel to every 20 grey squirrels in Britain.

BLUE POO!

Pine martens eat mice, birds, eggs, insects and fruit. In the summer they eat so many blaeberries (bilberries) that their poo turns blue!

DAD DANCER

The male capercaillie (ka-per-kay-lee) dances and sings to attract a female, making gurgling, wheezing and popping sounds.

SNEAKY STASHERS

Squirrels do not hibernate in winter. They store nuts and cones in the ground to eat when food is scarce.

STRUGGLE TO SURVIVE

The capercaillie became extinct in Scotland 250 years ago and was reintroduced. Most of its pine-forest habitat has been cut down, so it may become extinct in Scotland again.

Night Stalkers

TWIT–TWOO

Tawny owls are famous for their twit-twoo call, which we hear when the male and female birds call to each other. The female calls 'ke-wick' and the male answers 'hoo-hoo-oo'.

POWERFUL PREDATORS

Wildcats only come out at night. They have excellent night vision, and strong bodies for sprinting and pouncing on their prey.

EXCELLENT EARS

The brown long-eared bat is very quiet – there's no need to shout when you can hear so well.

STAR SPOT

WONDERFUL SCOTTISH WILDCAT

Wildcats used to live all over Britain until the forests they lived in were cut down, people hunted them, and they started breeding with pet cats. Now only 300 live in the Scottish Highlands and they are one of Scotland's most endangered species.

WOOLLY BEARS

Garden tiger caterpillars have the nickname 'woolly bears'. They are too hairy for most animals to eat.

MINI BAT

The common pipistrelle bat lives all over Scotland. It is tiny and weighs less than a 2p coin.

DON'T EAT ME!

Watch out, bats, the garden tiger moth is poisonous. Its bright colours say, 'Don't eat me!'

INSECT EATER

A pipistrelle bat eats 3,000 insects a night, which it hunts by using high-pitched squeaks and echolocation – like dolphins and whales.

BADGER BUFFET

A badger can eat 200 worms a night! Their thick skin and long, sharp claws mean they can also eat prickly hedgehogs.

SETTLE DOWN

Badgers live in an underground home called a sett. They often tidy up by carrying out old bedding, like dry grass and ferns, under their chin.

Rivers and Lochs

Scotland has over 3,000 freshwater lochs that were carved out of the landscape by huge glaciers in the Ice Age.

PITLOCHRY SALMON LADDER

Every year 5,000 Atlantic salmon and sea trout swim upriver through a specially built 'ladder' to avoid a hydroelectric dam. On their way back out to sea, young fish swim through the fish-friendly turbine blades of the power station — like a revolving door!

LOCH GARTEN OSPREYS

Ospreys became extinct in Scotland 100 years ago because of hunting and people stealing their eggs. Then a breeding pair flew over from Scandinavia in the 1950s and nested by Loch Garten! Ospreys have nested there every summer since.

Loch Ness holds more water than all the lakes in England and Wales put together, and legend says a famous monster lives there.

River Spey

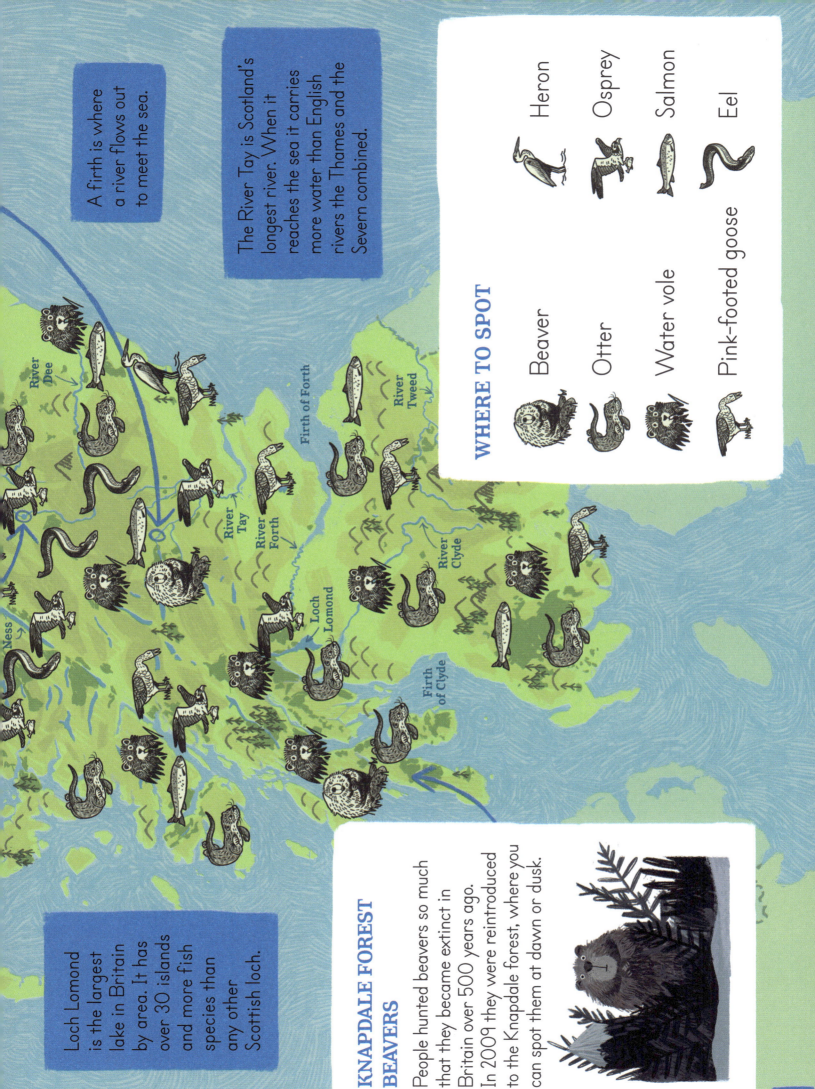

A firth is where a river flows out to meet the sea.

The River Tay is Scotland's longest river. When it reaches the sea it carries more water than English rivers the Thames and the Severn combined.

WHERE TO SPOT

Beaver

Otter

Water vole

Pink-footed goose

Heron

Osprey

Salmon

Eel

River Dee

Ness

River Tay

River Forth

Firth of Forth

River Tweed

Loch Lomond

River Clyde

Firth of Clyde

Loch Lomond is the largest lake in Britain by area. It has over 30 islands and more fish species than any other Scottish loch.

KNAPDALE FOREST BEAVERS

People hunted beavers so much that they became extinct in Britain over 500 years ago. In 2009 they were reintroduced to the Knapdale forest, where you can spot them at dawn or dusk.

Busy Riverbanks

HARD-HEADED
Great spotted woodpeckers have super-strong beaks, which they use to dig for insects, carve nesting holes and drum on tree trunks to attract a mate. They also have shock-absorbing skulls!

BIG BIRD
The grey heron is the tallest bird in Britain, at 1 metre tall. A group of herons is called a 'siege'.

STATUE STILL
Herons stand very still in shallow waters, waiting patiently to snap up fish, crayfish, small mammals and waterbirds with their long beaks.

STAR SPOT

BRILLIANT BEAVERS
Beavers belong to the rodent family, along with rats, mice, squirrels, hamsters and guinea pigs. They eat grass, leaves and tree bark. No other creatures in Scotland eat them.

EEL EXPLORERS

Adult eels leave Scottish rivers to lay their eggs in the Sargasso Sea – 3,000 miles away! Their eggs hatch into larvae that drift slowly back towards Europe, before growing into young eels that swim back upriver. But this epic journey has become harder for eels because of dams, over-fishing, pollution and climate change, and they are now critically endangered.

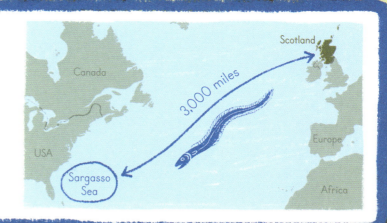

TOP OF THE MENU

Water voles are one of Britain's most endangered species. They taste so delicious that stoats, weasels, foxes, badgers, birds of prey, big fish and particularly American mink love to eat them.

ANIMAL ARCHITECTS

Beavers use their huge teeth to chop down trees, then dam rivers to make sheltered pools. There they build strong homes called 'lodges' out of branches, sticks and mud.

VOLE HIDEY-HOLE

Water voles build burrows with secret underwater entrances.

MY LIPS ARE SEALED!

Beavers have extra lips behind their teeth to keep water out while they gnaw wood underwater. They can hold their breath for up to 15 minutes!

SNAKING SCAVENGERS

Eels eat other fish, small creatures and even dead animals. They can live for up to 70 years.

Rushing Rivers

SUPER SALMON

The Atlantic salmon spends most of its life at sea, but it swims back to the river where it hatched to lay its eggs – a journey of up to 6,000 miles! Young salmon live in rivers for 6 years before swimming back out to sea.

FLYING FISH

An Atlantic salmon can jump 3 metres up waterfalls, dams and weirs to get back upstream to its home river.

SCUBA SWIMMERS

Otters are perfectly built for swimming, with webbed feet, waterproof fur, and ears and nostrils that can close underwater.

STRUGGLING SHELLFISH

Over half of the freshwater pearl mussels in the world live in Scotland. People have fished them for many years to harvest the beautiful pearls that can grow inside their shells, and now they are endangered.

POO CLUES
Otters are very hard to spot. Look for their pawprints and poos that smell like jasmine tea!

DIVING IN THE DARK
Kingfishers close their eyes as they dive into the water, and catch fish without looking.

STAR SPOT

OTTERLY AWESOME
More otters live in Scotland than anywhere else in Britain. They are one of Scotland's top predators, eating fish, waterbirds, frogs, toads and crabs, in rivers, lochs and the sea.

MASSIVE MUSSELS
Freshwater pearl mussels can grow as big as your hand and live for over 100 years!

Lively Lochs

STAR SPOT

AMAZING OSPREY
Ospreys are large birds of prey with a wingspan of 1 ½ metres – the size of a 12-year-old child. They nest in Scotland in summer and migrate south in winter.

GOGGLE EYES
Ospreys have an extra eyelid, which is see-through and protects their eyes underwater – like built-in goggles!

FISHING FEET
Ospreys hover high over lochs, rivers and firths and use their sharp eyesight to spot fish down below. They dive at high speed, plunging into the water feet first, to catch fish with their sharp talons.

BLOODSUCKERS
Only female midgies bite. They mostly drink blood from farm animals, but sometimes from people too! The males drink nectar from flowers.

DAMSEL IN DISTRESS
The northern damselfly is a super-rare insect that only lives around a few lochs and ponds in Scotland. Young damselfly larvae look like bugs and live beneath stones underwater.

THE DREADED HIGHLAND MIDGIE

Wings beat 1,000 times per second, faster than any creature in the world.

Wingspan just 2 millimetres, like a breadcrumb!

Short, sharp mandibles for biting.

SCOTTISH HOLIDAYS

Almost all the pink-footed geese in the world migrate to Britain in winter from their chilly nesting grounds in Iceland and Greenland. Many of them come to Scotland.

GOOD NEWS GEESE

Only 70 years ago pink-footed geese were endangered. Now there are over half a million birds worldwide, because they have been protected from hunting and shooting.

TOXIC TOAD

The warty skin of common toads produces a poison that puts other animals off eating them. They can also puff themselves up to scare off predators.

Grasslands

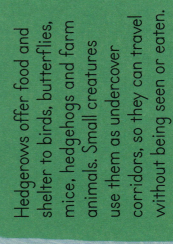

Hedgerows offer food and shelter to birds, butterflies, mice, hedgehogs and farm animals. Small creatures use them as undercover corridors, so they can travel without being seen or eaten.

SHETLAND PONIES

For 4,000 years Shetland ponies only lived on the Shetland Islands, where they adapted to suit the cold, wet, windy weather. They have short legs and thick coats but are strong and tough. More than 1,500 ponies live on the Shetland Islands today.

One third of Scotland is covered in grass!

MARVELLOUS MACHAIR

Machair (mack-er) is a Gaelic word for special grasslands on the north-west coast and islands of Scotland. Machair can have 45 different species of wildflower growing in just 1 square metre. It is also home to wading birds like corncrakes, as well as Britain's rarest bee, the great yellow bumblebee.

Most of Scotland's grassland is farmed. There are nearly 2 million cattle in Scotland and 6½ million sheep!

SCOTTISH SNAKES

Adders live on heaths, moors and in woods all over Scotland, but they are very hard to spot. They hibernate for nearly half the year and are extremely shy. They like to sunbathe in hot weather, so look out for snakes in the summer!

When too much land is farmed, there isn't enough natural habitat left for wild animals, birds and insects, and they struggle to survive.

WHERE TO SPOT

Shetland pony

Highland cow

Adder

Wild goat

Common lizard

Brown hare

Yellowhammer

Marsh fritillary butterfly

Marvellous Meadows

PUTRID PELLETS
Owls swallow their food whole and cough up the bits of fur and bone they can't digest in owl pellets.

DAY OWL
Unlike most owls, barn owls hunt in the daytime as well as at night. Their hearing is more sensitive than any other animal, helping them find hidden mice and voles.

STAR SPOT

BONNY BUTTERFLY
Marsh fritillary caterpillars only eat one plant (devil's-bit scabious), which sheep also like to eat. Most of their natural habitat has been turned into farms, so these butterflies are now endangered, with only about 35 colonies left in Scotland.

BOXING BROWN HARES
In spring, female brown hares fight off any males they don't want to mate with. They box each other with their front paws and pull out tufts of fur.

PINCHING FINCH

500 years ago, English King Henry VIII declared bullfinches to be criminals for stealing fruit from his orchards. He passed an Act of Parliament to reward people with one penny for every bird they killed.

MINI MINERS

Shetland ponies first left their islands around 200 years ago to pull heavy trucks through low underground tunnels in coal mines across Britain. They replaced women and children who used to do that work! Now these famous ponies live all over the world.

CHEESY SINGERS

Listen out for the yellowhammer's distinctive song, which sounds like, 'A little bit of bread and no cheese!'

PEOPLE'S PONIES

Although Shetland ponies look very wild, they are all looked after by people.

Hillside Home

SURVIVAL SKILLS

Highland cows are native to Scotland, but they are descended from the first cattle brought to Europe from Asia by Stone Age farmers over 4,000 years ago. Their hair is long, thick and waterproof to keep out the cold, wet, windy Highland weather.

SNAKE WRESTLING

Male adders fight to win over a female, twisting together in what looks like a dance, then wrestling each other to the ground.

BERRY RARE BEES

Mountain (or bilberry) bumblebees are specially adapted to living in high mountains, but they are becoming rarer because of climate change.

RARE REPTILES

Unlike other reptiles, adders and common lizards don't lay eggs. They both give birth to live young. They hibernate from October to March in fallen trees or old rabbit burrows.

GIDDY GOATS

Goats are usually farm animals, but some herds have been living wild in Scotland for hundreds of years, since many crofters left the country during the Highland Clearances.

EXPERT EATERS

Highland cows can graze steep mountainsides, eating tough, prickly plants that other animals avoid and digging through the snow with their horns to find buried plants.

STAR SPOT

ADDER ATTACK

The adder is Britain's only venomous snake. Its bite can kill small mammals, ground-nesting birds and lizards, but it hardly ever hurts people.

TAIL TRICKS

The common lizard can shed its whole tail to distract an attacker. The tail keeps moving while the lizard escapes! Then it can grow another one.

Why are animals in danger?

WATER POLLUTION

When chemicals and waste from farming and factories find their way into natural habitats like rivers and oceans, animals are poisoned and their habitats are damaged.

OVER-FISHING

Some fishing boats scoop up too many fish, which reduces their numbers to dangerous levels and leaves other sea creatures without enough food. Huge trawler nets damage the ocean floor.

PLASTIC POLLUTION

The world's oceans are full of plastic, which sea creatures swallow or get trapped in.

HUNTING

Some creatures have been hunted to extinction in Scotland for their meat, fur, eggs, to protect farm animals, or for sport. Some of these creatures have returned, but hunting is still a threat to many.

HABITAT DESTRUCTION

When people destroy wild spaces like forests to make room for farmland or towns, animals have nowhere to live and no food to eat.

ALIEN ANIMALS

When people release animals from other countries into the wild, they are known as 'alien' animals. They can take over habitats, eat all the food and bring new diseases.

CLIMATE CRISIS

Our planet is warming up, causing all wild habitats to change. Sea levels are rising and there are more storms, floods, droughts and fires. The climate crisis is a huge threat to all wildlife.

People have caused all these problems, but we can fix them too.

Turn the page to see how you can help!

How to help local wildlife

BUILD A BUG HOTEL

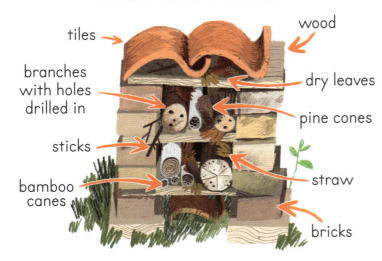

tiles

wood

branches with holes drilled in

dry leaves

pine cones

sticks

straw

bamboo canes

bricks

Recycle as much waste as possible, so it doesn't pollute natural habitats and hurt animals.

MAKE A BIRDBATH

A heavy rock will keep the bath steady

Old tray or shallow dish

Clean water for birds to drink and bathe in

Make a home for hedgehogs, frogs, toads, spiders and insects from a pile of branches, sticks and leaves.

Try to use less plastic. An apple core takes 2–3 months to rot away into nutritious soil, but a crisp packet takes up to 800 years!

GROW BEE-FRIENDLY FLOWERS AND HERBS

lavender

marigold

chive

oregano

forget-me-not

MAKE A BIRD FEEDER

string

plastic bottle

feeding holes in bottle

wooden skewers

seeds

dried oats

unsalted nuts

Walk, cycle or scoot when you can – it's healthy for you and for our planet!

How to spot wildlife

WHAT TO BRING

Rucksack

Water bottle

Snacks

Sun hat

Binoculars (if you have them)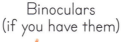

Wellies or walking boots

Waterproof jacket

FOLLOW THE COUNTRYSIDE CODE

- Only look for animals in places you're allowed to go.
- Take an adult with you.
- Stay a safe distance away from large animals like deer or cows.
- Leave gates as you found them, usually closed.
- Check the weather forecast, and the tide times if you are exploring by the sea.
- Do not disturb any wildlife or its home.
- Do not pick wildflowers or funghi.
- Take all your litter home.

WILDLIFE IS ALL AROUND YOU

Look for songbirds in trees and hedges.

Look for minibeasts under stones in a garden or park.

Look for ducks and swans around a canal or pond.

Want to discover more of AMAZING Scotland?

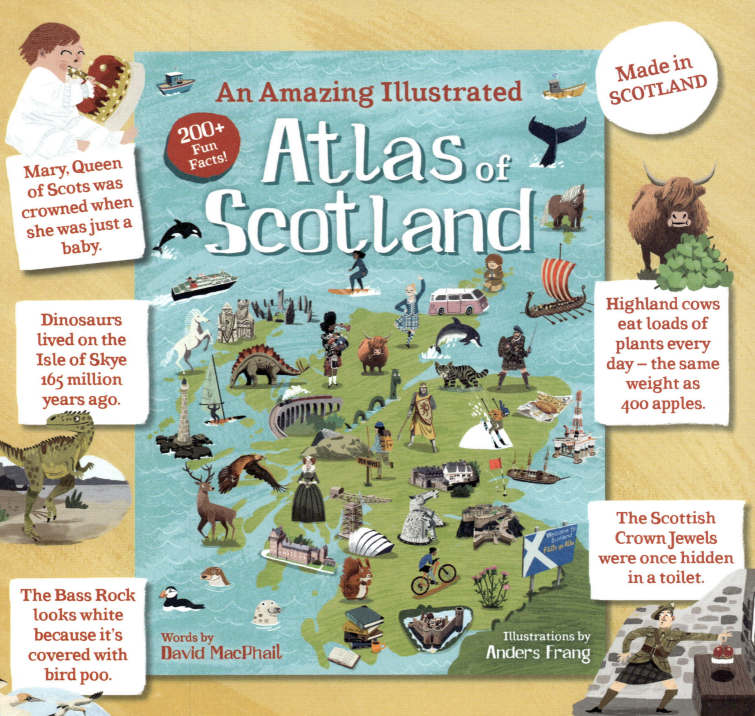

An Amazing Illustrated

Atlas of Scotland

200+ Fun Facts!

Made in SCOTLAND

Mary, Queen of Scots was crowned when she was just a baby.

Dinosaurs lived on the Isle of Skye 165 million years ago.

The Bass Rock looks white because it's covered with bird poo.

Highland cows eat loads of plants every day – the same weight as 400 apples.

The Scottish Crown Jewels were once hidden in a toilet.

Words by **David MacPhail**

Illustrations by **Anders Frang**

Discover fascinating facts about the people, places, history and culture that make Scotland so amazing.

DiscoverKelpies.co.uk